INVASION OF THE SHADOW PEOPLE

POEMS BY KEVIN RIDGEWAY

Luchador Press
Big Tuna, TX

Copyright © 2022, Kevin Ridgeway

First Edition: 1 3 5 7 9 10 8 6 4 2

ISBN: 978-1-958182-07-9

LCCN: 2022940196

Author photo: Kevin Ridgeway

Cover and title page art: Nikolai Lutohin

Acknowledgments:

Some of the poems herein previously appeared in the following journals:

Slipstream, Chiron Review, Nerve Cowboy, Main Street Rag, San Pedro River Review, Sheila-Na-Gig, Ghost City Review, The Cape Rock, Trailer Park Quarterly, Up the River, Nixes Mate Review, The Lake, Verdad, Poetic Diversity, Lummox, Big Hammer, Street Value, Moon Tide Press, MacQueen's Quinterly, Dryland, As it Ought to Be, Black Coffee Review, Fixator Press, Rusty Truck, Museum of Poetry, Live Nude Poems, Heroin Love Songs, Hobo Camp Review, Incandescent Mind, Gasconade Review, San Antonio Review, Picaroon Poetry, Suisun Valley Review, Drunk Monkeys, Good Works Review, Literary Orphans, Panoplyzine, Bank-Heavy, River City Poets, Vine Leaves, Olentangy Review, 48th Street Press, Suisun Valley Review and *Clutching at Straws.*

TABLE OF CONTENTS

FOR SANDRA

All I can do is be me, whoever that is.

-BOB DYLAN

MY DRUG DEALER CUT OFF MY HAIR

he was my barber
and my drug dealer
he cut up crystal into lines
with the same hands
he used to cut off
my locks
until they were
too short
for my dead mother
to recognize me in
my slenderized body
and a mind
burning from
the inside
and I was
no longer
her baby.

KING KONG vs. GODZILLA

my mother and I had epic battles:
her on one end of the house,
me on the other beating my chest,
drinking Steel Reserve and listening
to Warren Zevon at top volume
and my tirade of how she raised me
the wrong way was scoffed at in
disbelief at the amount of disrespect
I showed under her roof.
I roared to her that my life
was a mess because of her
shoddy parenting and she flipped out
and blew fire at me about how my brother
and I took her away from a possible
singing career, and she resented it
before saying I was just like her father
the flames spewing out her filterless
set of teeth which burned
the hair off of my chin
long enough for her to recognize
my baby face as I ooga ooga'd
to get my god-damned way--
there I said it, mother,
god-damn it!
my wife left me
for reasons I didn't want
to be blamed for.
so shut the hell up,
Mother, I said,

you've been talking
and not listening to me
for twenty three years.
now it's my turn,
you devil woman,
or I'm going to rocket
you back to the stoned age
when I smash this skyscraper
against your head
until you collapse on
a million fleeing people
like the ones
we both pushed away
who screamed
at the sight of us
as we loomed above
in an endless and futile war
where our lips didn't match
the words coming out of them.

I SURVIVED IKEA AND ALL I GOT WAS THIS LOUSY POEM

My girlfriend called a cab when
we were struggling to find the exit in
a labyrinth assembled with the hallmarks
of my Swedish heritage, Swedish
Christmas songs blasting in my ears
after I failed to finish my meat balls
over lunch and started having the biggest
panic attack of my life. She got me
outside and held my hand on our way
to the emergency room, where a doctor
told me that I had gravy on my mustache.
I felt well enough to lick it off at that
point and thanked him in the same
fractured language my grandmother
always spoke when she was too afraid
to teach me how she climbed out
of her pain long before her fire ever
went out and when we were unable
to reassemble her so we could feel safe
enough to reassemble ourselves.

TAKE A NUMBER

I am officially
declared insane
as I stand
on my head
in my underwear
and wait for
the blood
to rush
inside
my head
until it's so
heavy
it bursts
into a
million
different
faceless
statistics

LOOKING FOR LOVE
IN ALL OF THE WRONG PLACES

you're not my type
the homeless girl
outside of the 711
on Cherry Avenue
told me, a rude
and empty awakening
for my precarious
dawn time libido.
She sang
no you're never
gonna get it
before she ran off
into the shadows
with the five bucks
I had hoped would
give me permission
to rescue her
in the nightmare
of being lost
on filthy streets,
where humanity
is cheaper than
the desperation
for a love neither
one of us can find.

EAGLE ROCK

he took me up the steep hills
overlooking an old cemetery
where he was raised
and cracked open a
lukewarm can of beer
telling me of the times
he would race cars
and crash into parked ones
or the time he caught
his older brother's friend
fixing heroin
over the bathroom sink
and got his first taste
of forbidden fruit
he pointed out the
Laundromat where he
committed his
first robbery,
the burger stand
he fired his first gun in
the high school
he dropped out of .
when he got his
first prison sentence
he told me these things
and extinguished his
filter-less Camel

into the last dregs
of the beer
and asked me
if I wanted to
hear a scary story.

TOXIC MASCULINITY

My father never taught me anything
other than how to saw women in two
with electric charisma that leaves us
both daydreaming in separate prisons
and all of them dying while waiting
for us to join them on the outside.
He taught me how to break hearts
by way of the art of self destruction.
He taught me how to rob, cheat
and steal the pants off anyone
I could manipulate. He never
taught me how to drive a car
or how to ride a bike or how to fish.
I looked in his dusty dresser drawers
for artifacts that he left behind:
his 1983 wardrobe and his last
pack of camel non filters,
half of it smoked on the day
he was captured, the other half
brittle with straws of tobacco
which tasted like a very bitter
kind of silly string that is
anything but silly
and is killing him as
he battles lung cancer
in prison. He taught me
the power of mystery
and the art of disappearing.
But it all has gone down

like a movie:
one big mushroom cloud
of devastation as we drift
further into the darkness
that my father taught me.

PRISON WIVES

They are all scattered
about the seaside waiting area,
applying last minute touches
of makeup and straightening
their pantyhose. One by one,
we enter the security checkpoint.
We stare at the guard in disbelief
when he commands our mother
to remove her brassiere after
its underwire sets off
the metal detector. They hold
it up for all to see like a prize
or a Ripley's Believe it or Not
oddity before they grant us access
to the next security checkpoint
across a concrete bridge
closer and closer to
a bittersweet family reunion
beyond the chicken wire,
my father in tears
while I bounce around in his lap
and in the blink of an eye
they take him back
passed the iron doors
after he makes out
with my mother
in a frenzy
of desperate passion
while the inmate

next to us sticks his hand
under his wife's dress
in front of their children,
and her eyes roll into
the back of her head.

THE 1983 HOME SECURITY SYSTEM

on a night like this one, thirty years ago
the family settled down to bed after an evening
at the cinema taking in Return of the Jedi
when the sound of smashing glass
echoed through the house
the noise of an intruder fumbling
in the living room stunned my folks awake
and my father could find no weapons
in the dark of the bedroom
save for a handful of his belts
gleaming in the dim light
of the walk-in closet
he leaped out from the shadows
attired in only his boxers
swinging the belts in every direction
screaming in a strange gibberish
that horrified the burglar
and my father chased him ninja-style
down the street like this until
the man disappeared around the
corner of the street in terror.
no one ever broke into the house again,
but over time the old man was gone
leaving it up to me to carry out his legacy:
so I sit here under the shadows in my boxers,
my arsenal of belts at my side
waiting for the underbelly of society
and, despite many false alarms
running half naked in the streets

and getting arrested for disturbing the peace
this system has worked
and our few valuables were all safe
under the watchful guard
of crazy white boys in their underwear
screaming at bad guys to get the hell
away from what they loved the most.

LOST HOME MOVIES

His smooth, charismatic voice
broke up the static of the collect calls
he sent my mother from
a minimum security federal prison
most days after I got out of school.
He tripped out on the fact that
he created me with his seed.
He also broke the news to me
the night before my tenth birthday
that I'd never be nine years old again,
and that I was closer to the end
of all that we can see or dream.
I was proud to no longer believe
in Santa and the Tooth Fairy,
yet I believed the lies
they all told me of my
father's heroism in an unjust world
that took him away from us.
He charmed my mother long enough
for her to find the good buried inside of him,
before he fooled her for all eternity, and
I'll never have another father to fool me again.

GRANDMA GOES TO REHAB

I was six years old and told by my uncle
that we were going on a treasure hunt
through grandma's house, and if I found
all the empty bottles of vodka, there
would be a prize! a seasoned excavation
artist from my previous seasons looking
for Easter eggs, I found everything from
pints to gallons; some of them had exotic
labels with strange Russian names, others
had familiar supermarket iconography,
and I scored extra points plus
a pat on the head when I discovered
one lingering underneath the wig
that sat atop her dresser. And
as I watched him empty every flask
and airplane shooter, I thought
to myself that grandma sure
was thirsty and must be having a
wonderful time at camp because
she had been there for weeks.
I would come to understand
the purpose of all of this years later
when there was a treasure hunt
held in my room in the garage.
I packed my bags, bottles falling
out of garbled shirts that I stuffed
into a worn suitcase, my family
sending me off to "camp" like
dear old grandma twenty years

and several cocktails earlier to
dry out and have a treasure hunt
through the twisted psyche
of my bitter inheritance.

BE CAREFUL WHAT YOU WISH FOR

My father had finally come home
after twelve years in a federal penitentiary.
It was the first birthday I spent
with both of my parents.
The day I became a teenager.
My brother had moved out of the house
three months before,
so I had them both all to myself.
We decided to visit Forest Lawn
in the hills overlooking
the movie studios, where
we paid our respects to
the dead movie stars
who I worshipped with
the hope that I would escape
from my lonely childhood,
at a time when
black and white ghosts
kept me company, and when
I discovered who my parents
pretended to be before
they both became ghosts who
watched me grow up in the dark
in search of them all, in a place
where dreams go to die.

ABOVE THE RUBBLE

When I was thirteen years old, my older brother
moved out of the house; before he boarded that
Greyhound bus to his freedom in the American
south, he took me on a walk through our old
neighborhood. We saw all of the couches
resting on overgrown lawns while stepping
over the shattered glass of a million half-drunk
beer bottles, the cracked pavement stained by
amber ale and vomit. We walked around the
parameter of this lower class wasteland and saw
the empty strip malls playing host to drug deals,
insane homeless men living in shopping carts
and aimless gang-bangers smoking speed in
parked cars; my brother told me that we both
had to get out of this place and never look back.
He never returned to live in the mire of the
old neighborhood. I managed to get away long
enough to see the world and ruin
my early adult life and was dragged back
to this place kicking and screaming.
I'm still stuck here, eternally in
between trains. As I sit here on the front
patio of my childhood home, polishing off
a cup of instant coffee and extinguishing my
cigarette on the asphalt, gunshots in the distance
and police helicopters hovering above. I close
my eyes and dream myself far away from this
cul de sac of evolving monstrosities. I dream
of it being torched to the ground and replaced
by a green field of endless trees. I can run toward
my dreams and never look back again in anger.

DAD WAS A NEEDLE HYPE

we listened to the Stones
in my Dad's Ford Ranchero
after he got kicked out of rehab
during a thunderstorm
in Long Beach, CA,
on our way back to
my mother's house
to beg her to give him
another chance. It was
the first time he told me
about heroin, and why
he would never be free.

THE BOY WITH THE HIDDEN DISEASE

My mother sent me to therapy
after I returned from theater camp,
where I met girls for the first time
a place where I basked in the
freedom of popularity and friendship
before it was all sucked away
and she drove me back into
the solitary adolescent dungeon
of my hidden lair in the garage.
No one spoke to me once
the bells rang back at school,
where I melted back into a loser.
My new therapist was the father
of one of the varsity cheerleaders
from my high school. She would
bump into me in the waiting room,
awkward in her efforts to ignore me
until she whispered my identity
to classmates who all knew
I was a basketcase. Her father
tried to sell me a series of books
he'd written about the masks
people wear in order to keep up
with the joneses in our stubborn
lies of perfection. I was no longer
the kid everyone loved, whose
Dennis the Menace fashion sense
assured them all that he had yet
to grow a penis. I replaced him

with a whiny, manic abomination
of hormones, great expectations
and too much designer imposter
cologne, in an endless, psychotic
rehearsal that I hoped would win me
freedom in my wildest dreams
of a world where everyone would
confess their insanity long enough
in their attempts to be my friends.

FLASH FLOOD WARNING

I am walking down Pacifc Coast Highway
in a gnarly downpour of endless rain
with water levels rising to where
the end of the gutter meets
the beginning of a slippery sidewalk
scarred by cracks from years
of hard street life hitting its pavement
but not from little old me
with the umbrella that breaks
halfway during my trip
to the local mental health clinic
when a car full of undergraduate girls
splashes toxic rain water all over me
in a tidal wave of muddy flth
and I run after their car until
I realize who was guilty of splashing me
a bunch of girls laughing at me
and mouthing that they were sorry
as they splashed me again
making a California turn onto
Cherry Avenue on their way
to dry classrooms and younger
versions of me soaking wet
from similar incidents on
the way to school, fellows
who those girls laugh at
and fellows who write poems
about those mean girls
who didn't mean it every time

they said they were sorry to us
when we asked them out on dates
that ended at 6 PM, but I don't
take shit from girls like that
anymore, and I threw my
umbrella in the direction
of their moving car and flipped
them of until they screamed
out the back window that I was
just another stupid ass white boy,
but I never gave up screaming
angry gibberish at them while
people looked on from their
cars and wondered if I was
crazy or high, or just plain
fucking tired of being so
goddamned down on my luck
and standing here, all alone
with all eyes on me.

LOCAL G

"I've been gangbangin' since
I was a juvenile,"
the high-wired figure said
from the dark over a
chain link fence
at my friend
Don Juan's,
his face scarred
from acne
his hair cut
from a soup bowl
and his teeth
gnashing
as he moved
back and forth
in Bruce Lee kicks
ready to ask
me what the
fuck you
lookin' at,
white boy?

MY NEIGHBOR'S BACKYARD

he pulls a cart along the busy boulevard
full of bottles and cans collected
from dumpsters and private garbage
I hear the clash of broken glass and
dented aluminum in his backyard
next door; I peak over the fence
and a waft of methamphetamine
smoke hits me in the face while
decline, watching the eyes in his
head swim his pupils trying to
hairy beach of his salt-and-pepper
last dregs of a forty ounce
King Cobra, a cigarette butt
dancing at the bottom
I just stare at him for a moment,
standing beneath an unruly
tree of uneaten lemons and
a plagued stench of fruit flies.
I move back to clean my
own mess, suds against
the sins please wash away.

HIP, SLICK AND COOL

I was so cool one night
at a dorm party at the start
of freshman year, but
I could not remember
how to be cool like
that again. I drank
and smoked and
snorted in search
of the hip cat
everyone was
talking about.
I thought I had them
all fooled into believing
that I had life
all figured out
until they all told me
about the man
they met the night
before, who surprised
them when he numbed
every painful feeling
and replaced them
with the hungover
delusion that I was
smooth enough
to never let any
of them down
like my trousers
were at a party

where I failed
to inspire them
to grow up so
they could all
be just like me.

TWO GUYS SPEAKING
GIBBERISH TO THEMSELVES

They pace up and down
opposing sides of the street
talking gibberish out loud
to themselves, in danger
of being popped by the fuzz
until me and another vagabond
move the two men to face
each other as though they
are having a conversation,
and then somebody sells them
a bag of methamphetamine
which surrounds them with
a crowd of invisible demons
who tear them apart.

THE FRACTURED PORCELAIN OF
A DEMENTED ANGEL

we were both admitted the night before
her porcelain smile lighting the hangover of the am hallways
from a wheelchair after she plowed her car into a phone pole
in an attempt to end her life and I told her I just got suicidal
and had taken too much benadryl which made her laugh
and laugh and laugh. She spun her wheelchair all over me,
eager for the first morning smoke break, and that's when
she rolled us up, lit us up and smoked us both.

FOR THE GIRL WITH MY DEAD GIRLFRIEND'S NAME

Her sad eyes plead with me
for more of my story
after I processed some of my grief
in group therapy in a suburban psych ward
I've not been to before, and the only way
I can avoid breaking both our troubled hearts
is to not say another word.

PINK CLOUD

a jittery guy with armpit
sweat stains who just got out of
the hospital after filleting his wrists
said he had two weeks of sobriety,
and that everything was great, had
never been better, almost annoyingly
so. he got his family back and was
even kayaking again. days later, he
relapsed on an Ambien-tequila cocktail
and was sent back to inpatient treatment,
having fallen out of the sky after
getting burned by an angry sun that
sent him down to earth in fumes
where all of his unsolved problems
remained after he fooled himself
into thinking he'd be spared of
those cruel vultures as they resumed
a long and insane feast of a man
with psychic mazes inside of him
too afraid to stumble through to the
other ends of confrontation with
his dark shadows to earn that ray of
healing light very few can bathe
themselves under in their efforts
to part the wicked storm clouds
of insidious self deception.

THE MAN WITH THE
MAD SCIENTIST'S HAIRCUT

uses natural product:
his brains got paranoid
enough to crawl out
of his waxen ears
to lick two cones
of frizz
on two ends
of a bald coffee-tanned
middle dome full
of wasted invention.

THE REMAINS OF MY FATHER

I picked up a bust my mother
made of my incarcerated father's head.
I threw it against her 1960's tile kitchen floor,
and it shattered into a million different pieces.
I gazed at my trembling hands and
licked the blood across my knuckles
after I broke my parents' hearts
with my revenge killing. I've endured
many sleepless nights draped in
a heavy guilt that has left me drenched
in a kind of shame reserved for tainted
angelic boys with the same conscience
that tortured my mother at her
every mistake. I grew up to poison
myself until I transformed
into a supernatural monster
from a place much worse than
any of the kinds of perceived hell's
they failed to scare me straight with
in order to embrace the false promise
of an indifferent heaven,
a heaven that took away
our lost souls and shattered them
all into a million different pieces.

FLOATING ON THE PALE BACKSIDE
OF DEATH

One summer after he was paroled,
my father and I decided to fill
our empty swimming pool with
garden hose water. We both
performed handstands in secondhand
swim trunks and talked about
going to Forest Lawn Cemetery
to check out the celebrity graves
that afternoon. We soon
blasted out of the driveway
in his vintage El Camino,
both of us still damp from
jumping off the diving board
and into a shallow sea
of filthy water. We were on
our way to the cocktail party
of dead celebrities, all of them
hidden behind marble
and under the imported grass
of surrounding hillsides.
They were our best friends
because they never talked back
or dared to even judge us,
and they always saved the day
with a glamour that made
us drown in our attempts
to escape from the low-class
prison we found ourselves in
off screen, both of us missing
on the cutting room floor.

WHEN I GREW TALL ENOUGH
TO SEE BEHIND MY FATHER'S EYES

I had finally heard a song
that expressed my wordless mind
and my wordless feelings.
I can't remember what it was called,
but it was mean, sleazy, and sung
by Mick Jagger. I first heard it
in the passenger seat of a stolen Cadillac
my father hot wired in a grocery store
parking lot.   We drove around
Rancho Palos Verdes and those
big green hills loomed in quiet mystery
over the violent and unforgiving waves
of the Pacific Ocean, a primal scream
over smoking guitars and a growl of pain,
to a secluded alcove on the private beach
we broke into and we both screamed
when our flesh hit that water to freeze
our shared blood, a primordial howl
into a setting sun where I discovered
my father's broken dreams
and I began to swim in them
until we were both on the shore
and he whispered into my ear
words I will never repeat,
words that are mine to remember
when we both shared hope
before he disappeared
and his voice greeted me again

in the static fray of a collect call
from a faraway penitentiary
to apologize for a future
when I would be standing
out there on that beach alone.

PAROLE VIOLATIONS

he taught me how to pick the locks
on car wash vacuum machines in order
to loot them for quarters we could use
for a payphone call to my mother
when we had to abandon his maroon
1979 Ranchero in the middle of a busy
intersection after it ran out of gas on our
way home from the methadone clinic

we waited for her to come pick us up
and we split my first beer that he used
to swallow all the painkillers he had
stolen, his red flannel Pendleton shirt
folded over a bulging forearm scarred
by prison murals that whispered dirty
words to me that I didn't know before
and haven't heard since

DUMPSTER DIVE

Dad procured a dildo
one night past twelve
when he was tweaking
and searching for used
parts to operate a used
microwave oven that
he intended to transform
into a television set
that cooked tv dinners
against the swollen
faces of dead actors
still alive in reruns
like the reruns of
insanity my father
kept repeating each
night until his eyes
swam away from
his dilated head.

GETTING HIGH WITH MOM AND DAD

My mother started to look
and talk like a melting
Salvador Dali painting
when my father came to
in hand-me down David Koresh
eye glasses. My mother
held the pot smoke in her lungs
and passed the lit joint
to my father. He let my mother
shotgun clouds of weed smoke
in the middle of a kiss
and before I knew it,
they both agreed how trippy
it was that I came from
my father's testicles.
They bushwacked
and zoned out while
they tripped out
and fingered
the curly hair of my
long beard to hide
a baby face they
grew nostalgic about.
My mother started
laughing because
she thought my face
looked like a vagina.
The high soon wore off,
and we were awkward

and distant with each
other all over again.
My mother asked me
at one point if I had
any more weed. I lied
when I told her no.

THE WIFE OF THE LATE BLOOMER BANDIT

It has been brought to my attention
that my father is dying
of lung cancer behind prison walls
they put him behind again and again
after he made the front page
of the local newspaper
as the mastermind
of three bank robberies
that shamed my mother
who did not live in freedom
as she waited for him
to come home
and make things right
for all of us to be together
in love while our dreams
came true and justice
was finally served
but it looks a lot different
when you see through all
its ugliness as you let him
slowly fade away when all
he wanted to do was be
among the ones
who all burned out
into an endless night where
my dead mother no longer dreams.

MY FATHER IS DYING IN PRISON AND
HE NEEDS BETTER MEDICINE

He is given codeine
after a career as an armed robber
to supported a heroin habit
that escalated when my parents
found out that I was on the way
he wanted her to abort me
which he now regrets saying
but with lung cancer ravaging
his body, no flimsy dose of codeine
is going to numb his physical pain
and the invisible psychological pain
of his double dragon mind
and I wish there was a way
to smuggle drugs into him
so he can go out in comfort
I don't care if he dies by the needle
he chose the needle over us
so many endless times
he thought would be different
just like I experience so many
endless bottoms until I learn
not to pull the triggers
so I have another excuse
to numb my lack of any real pain to kill
like the pain that is killing my father.

SON OF THE LATE BLOOMER BANDIT

The cops raided our house
and my parents were both taken
to jail. I had no choice but to
identify my father
in surveillance videos.
I was subpoenaed
by the district attorney.
I sat in the echoing marble halls
of the courthouse
across from the young bank tellers
he terrorized, both of them girls
my age who glared at me
when they recognized
his sinister face in mine.
My testimony helped
send my father to prison
for the rest of his life.
It's been ten years
and now my mother
is dead and no longer held
captive in the epic misery,
of his fiendish lifelong search
for a chemical escape.
He said heroin made him
closer and unafraid of death,
numb to his own doom.
They announced his
life sentence on the front page
of the local newspaper, my
name was never mentioned.

They did not want to believe
he had a son who
was more dangerous
to them with deep wounds
gone unhealed. I will kidnap
their fathers if I ever decide
to return to claim
what they all robbed
from me. I will be
reunited with
my father in prison,
where we will start
a massive riot to burn
the walls down, He
and I will escape from
the smoking rubble
back into a world
where people tried
to throw us all away

THE LAST TIME I SAW MY FATHER'S FACE

My father
was bearded
and zoned out
on psychiatric medication
he could not pronounce
behind the glass from us
in county jail,
where he awaited trial.
He and my mother
argued over
why he did what he did
until he could only
slur insane gibberish.
The guards treated us
so much like shit
we could still smell it
on the drive home,
when we both agreed
never to visit my father
in jail or prison again.
Neither of my parents
were there when I got
locked up in the same
madhouse that swallowed
my father whole,
but it choked on me
and spit me out
in a demented miracle
no one prayed for but me.

THE BEGINNING OF FOREVER

she had a
brain aneurysm
and she kept saying
to the paramedics
I'm okay, I'm okay
when I got the call
I knew it was the end,
because she spent
so much time
and energy
during her
last year alive
trying to explain
to me with
her final breaths
that she had
little time left,
and I had better
get my
shit together
we all watched
her slowly
fade away
in a hospital
overlooking
Sunset Boulevard,
her mind bleeding,
gone. and my
insanity still unfolding.

INVASION OF THE SHADOW PEOPLE

sunken ghost faces linger in the dark
while we scratch our faces
for imaginary bugs from street drugs,
and everything we thought we learned
from our past depravity
to whose core we came toward
after we began to dig deeper
beyond the limits of that everything,
and I tell myself it's the chemicals
in my brain swirling it into
a paranoid shipwreck of memory loss
and old daydreams
that will never come true.
The hallucinatory midnight demons
carried them all the way to hell
that I only saw when I hallucinated
with a mind full of Christian guilt
for trying to cheat God
and Mother Nature, who both
conjured up my worst nightmares
in the middle of their tough love for me
as they taught me not to worship
at the altar of my dangerous mind.

BIPOLAR #1

I finally placed first in
something, a twin headed
dragon diagnosis whose flames
I ran away from for years
before the Merry-go-Round
inside of my skull began to
spin out of control. My parents
pulled me out of my charred ruins
when I finally became frightened
of it all enough, a grave dug
to bury myself in unpaid
student loans, a divorce
and more failures soiled
in premature dirt, after I'd
become twisted enough
gazing at the distorted
mirrors of my funhouse mind,
when it still wasn't cool to be
so mercurial in temperament
in sociology classroom outbursts,
naked in public and in
cruel pursuit of the man
hiding in every reflection,
hiding in a crippled obscurity
as they harness all these
painful daydreams I've
had to learn to swim in
from rains imagined
by an indifferent sky.

FLESHY MITTEN JITTERS

My fingers are invisible at the rate they're traveling at,
and I usually miscalculate whenI attempt to applaud
with the hands they sprouted from. When trying to
give someone a High Five, I usually miss, slapping
them in the face. It's not all clumsiness, it's neurons
colliding inside my scratched phonograph record brain,
my lithium salted nervous system not responding when
I want to reach out to touch something or someone,
and the flutter of this defective pair of butterfly claws
always turns me into a wounded beast that cannot
learn to hold on without breaking from the unwieldy
curse of a low budget horror movie tremor that purrs
wearily inside the rapid beat of its wrists.

KID BROTHER DROPOUT

I wanted to be just like my older brother;
tired of being known as just his kid brother,
so I wanted to be his equal or surpass him.
I auditioned for the same role he won awards
for my senior year but I lost the role to a friend.
And I was passed over by my brother's college,
an inferior little man in the shadows of the great one
I must bow to but instead I rebelled and became
a bearded freak in the green mountains of Vermont,
doing drugs and fueling my damaged little ego
with a new frontier of possibilities big brother
could never dream of after a slight bit
of chemical brain damage freed me of the need
to compare myself to him or want to kick him
in the eye with my cowboy boots wrestling him
on the living room carpet back in 1984
when I fought dirty and tried to bite his dick off,
still fighting dirty to this day in order to overcome
my lack of an identity after years of not knowing
who to be as the youngest in a family
composed of worldwide superstars

THE UGLY PARADE

it was a mountain college
tradition of ours. We were
societal outsiders with
a defiant spirit we believed
would conquer fascism.
They march single file
dressed in hideous costumes
to go with their distorted minds
down every snowy path
and through every single
dorm room, including
my girlfriend's room,
where she had
to cancel my blow job
for a bedside ticket
to these hideous
doo dah kids,
and one of them asked
my girlfriend if my penis
was big and ugly
or tiny and flaccid,
but she refused to answer
their questions and we turned
them away, having renounced
or own personal freakdom
for the false comfort
of mainstream exclusivity
where we were ejected
when we let them

all know how beautiful
we were on the outside
but on the inside,
we were uglier than
every last one of them.

JUNIOR HUSBAND

I was 21 years old
when I dressed in my
wife's underwear
and built a
studio apartment
altar to Steely Dan,
read Dostoevsky
and anything that
thumbed its nose
at the man.
I knew everything
and was about
to change the
world with my
diseased creative
laziness.
I drank tequila shots
in anonymity
behind paper bag masks
and I suffered forty hour weeks
as a counter jockey
where the politicians
picked up their prescriptions
and naked activists
tried to march away the war
ground zero was
still on fire
when she left me
after she went to

visit her father
who finally
convinced her
I was no good
and her last kiss
smashed my lips
into the back
of my wasted
little head.

COUNTY JAIL THANKSGIVING

the other inmates
dined in their cells at noon
once the deputies had shut off
the Macy's Parade in the dayroom,
where i remained handcuffed to
a cylinder made of iron
on a chair made from steel,
and the smiles of chipper
talking heads were pummeled
by a blizzard of static.

after my return to my cellmate,
i stared as boxcar wheels
shocked out electric ghost frowns
through the slit window as they
rolled around the hillside where
the Dodgers built a ballpark
altar to the gods inside rainclouds
who held the sun for ransom
behind a grief-stricken sky.

DINGS

That's what the deputies called us
in line at five am for court
in velcro stitched suicide gowns
that made us captive,
low-rent Roman warriors
"The dings behaved themselves
the most on this trip out of anybody"
one of them said to the other
and the inmates in general population
told us they were out for our blood
and I escaped with my ding mind
because I knew how to truly
shut the fuck up
or become somebody's
bitch hardcore and nasty,
another misunderstood face
in another broken crowd.

UNCHAINED

In the darkness of the iron LA County Sheriff's bus
night has fallen, and we're en route downtown
to Twin Towers Correctional Facility, my day in court
having awarded me my freedom after two weeks
as an inmate among hardcore OG's, pimps and hustlers
the truly afflicted men of the darkness, each of them
whooping and hollering from the rear cell benches
to the young women bound in steel cages up front
Nick, his face battered, the deputies boot marks
still visible across his forehead, his arm in a sling
busted and fucked up by the LAPD after a fast
rolling misadventure, crash landed after slamming
tweek; my head clearing, weeping over my impending
freedom, terrified: "Take your meds, bro," he told me
"and pray for me, brother, pray for my kids, man"
I squeezed his cuffed hand, the both of us bound
together in chains, our heads bound in prayer
he made me promise him I'd pray for his babies
everyday, and that's when I confessed to him
that my father spent my entire childhood in prison
and when I made the tough phone call to inform
him of my mother's tragic early demise, my father
confessed to me he'd lied to her and to me
he'd been sentenced to life in prison without parole.
and I'd likely never look deep into the tired,
relentless spark of my own father's eyes again.

THE SOUND OF UGLINESS

I was grateful to hear music
on the county jail bus
after weeks of listening
to my fellow inmates
screams in their battles
with the clubs and tear gas
from deputies who controlled
what we listened to on
our way to court when
GIMME SHELTER
pounded the iron bus,
a favorite song of my father's
who at the time was
serving a life sentence upstate.
When the deputy changed
the station over to country music,
that made us all too deaf to fight
over the sonic expression
of our rebellion from a society
that didn't want to give us
a chance in hell. We were
terrified of who the judge
might be and they could
have sentenced me
to a lifetime of silence
while I tried to remember
the songs I missed the most,
and not by so and so
while the deputy at the wheel
began to sing along.

One of my fellow inmates
told him to shut the fuck up.
The music was turned off
and the deputies came
into the back to beat
the living fuck out of him,
but he kept singing music
that is known
to kill fascists
like the ones
who strangled him
for all the joy he got
caught trying to steal
from everybody else
to soften the blow
of his miserable life,
in a world where
crooked pigs who
think they can sing.

BRAIN MATTER

chow time came
before the sun went
down on L.A. County Jail,
where people try
to trade shots
of instant coffee
for fruit in order to make pruno.
I had just been taken off
suicide watch and had been
stuffed into a yellow
mental health
smock for dings
like us or whatever else
the deputies laughingly called us.
Everyone's favorite meal
was called brain matter,
our tray canvasses
decorated in gray
hamburger and
a decadent brown
mystery sauce
over curly noodles.
We slurped from
other inmates' scraps
of a kind of meat
we couldn't beat
after lights out
and we all passed out
fat, happy and behind bars.

I started to almost miss
the god forsaken place
in the cab headed away
from downtown LA
en route to the suburb
where my uncle
reluctantly said
I could sleep
on his couch.
That night I had to start
proving that my brain
mattered more than
the way I treated it
with the disintegration
of what I was really made of:
the armor I inherited
with a straight poker face
and everything my father
taught me in his old prison
stories of bad food,
toilet hooch, racism,
murder, riots, lock down
and solitary confinement,
but he never mentioned
brain matter, which
I want to ask him
about while lung cancer
brings his life sentence
to a close as he digests
his last supper and the epic
wrongs of his life
over a glass of toilet hooch

he uses to forget and come
as close to death in hot pursuit
of the double dragon
who ran off with my
father's brain to another
place that doesn't matter.

WHEN HER FATHER THOUGHT I WAS
A DOPE FIEND

He looked at me with a screaming sunburn
courtesy of the Long Island sun.
He gasped and frightened me
from ever showing my face around
his house again, dressed in a cardigan
I stole from a young girl
who said she didn't love me back.
My arms were never visible
to authority figures dethroned
by my rejection of the lies
old people tell themselves
when they are too afraid
of young people like me
who aren't the devil
they thought we were underneath
all of the second hand layers,
surrounded by stacks of used books,
books which wrote out
my entire post-adolescent destiny
in the rebirth of a misguided rebellion
her father would never understand
in his search for needle hype
track marks he believed
I hid from him. I remained
stashed away in his
daughter's bedroom
during summer break
from a school

where we learned
that men like him ruled
a hateful past punks like me
were born to run away from.

TALKIN' PSYCH WARD BLUES

This time around there was no camaraderie
just a bunch of us bearded scraps of imbalance
bitter nurses and pretty social workers younger than me
asking me what my hobbies were
while I sat in my pajamas and I told them I wrote poetry
They didn't get my jokes and twitched
when they asked if I'd had a bowel movement that day
and I made a shit joke that got a shuddered response
But they got me on better meds. Clark Gable
and Joan Crawford kept me company on TV at night and
I realized I'm tired of being a manic depressive alcoholic,
but at least the schizophrenic dude next door to me
thought I had style in my bathrobe, called me a
smooth diamond in the rough, a fighter
and that he had hope for me and my raggedy ass
because sometimes when I spoke, it seemed awkward
but it also seemed tortured, tired and halfway real.

MINIATURE JESUS

"I spent the 1990's in jail because of the 1980's,"
short round Jesus looking homeboy spouts to me
and googly-eyed methamphetamine prophecy
slips right of his tongue through no teeth
his flip-flops smack his heels while he paces
the hallway at four thirty in the morning
alongside crippled little tired old fucking me
the two of us breaking the ice
after the voices he heard got quieter
and he praises the lord for ABC Channel 7
as it comes in and out of reception
OJ Simpson clips playing 25 years
after the big chase in our backyards
on the television in a common room
where we are lectured to by social workers
on healthy coping skills
and he cuts a loud fart
while he stands on his tip toes
to push decaf coffee out of an empty urn
before dousing it in twenty seven packets of sugar
the social worker deciding to cut the group short
as the funk settled in
the doctors make him stay longer
than they made me stay
but we slapped each other's backs
when I left, bag in hand
and his break dance moves
during nicotine patch upgrades
from surly medication nurses

who don't ever want
his spark plug warm
bleeding heart light
to leave them and that whole
indirect primal scream
of a madhouse like
I now have, the one-man
show to an audience of himself
in whispered non sequiturs,
all of them still echoing
in my locked-down mind.

SLOW BURN

that little bitch screamed,
wailed and threatened to
have the hospital staff
reported until the doctor
let her have the dose
of xanax that was to
her liking and the
American Spirit cigarettes
her parents dropped off
because she was so much
better than the generic brand
freebies the rest of us got
at smoke break, when
she took the longest
out of any of us
to finish up because
those Spirits burn slow,
like I do, until I explode
and become the same
little bitch that she was,
demanding and pointing
fingers and punching fists
until we got what we damn
well wanted, no matter
who got hurt and in the end
we were just sick, sad
and alone as the smoke
cleared away and even we
saw ourselves for what

we are. She told me to have
a nice life when I was
discharged, and to enjoy
a smoothie in her honor.
And I blended one flavored
with the same kind of insanity
we had a mutual taste for.

HAPPY MEAL

I was standing in line
at group therapy
waiting for powdered eggs
when someone finally
seemed to have more B.O.
than me, and a new patient
asked me if I was
an observer,
not a patient
just like I thought
my late girlfriend
was a counselor
and not a patient
at the same rehab
we met each other
in. Just like my
mother and her
mother found
their spouses
in rehab. But
I had little time
to ruminate
over all of this
when someone
farted what we
all thought to be
akin to a rotten egg
and, for a moment,
I was cured of
all my problems
outside of that one fart.

SHORT BUS CHOIR

I was sitting in the packed backseat
of the patient van for the local
mental health facility when a
fellow manic depressive yelled
at the driver to turn up the K-EARTH
and everyone began stuttering along
to B-B-B-Benny and the Jets
and, with the sun blinding me from
the windshield, I began my falsetto
solo at the finale. no one remembered
our singalong the next day, including me
in my antipsychotic haze when a
schizophrenic yelled at the driver to
turn up the K-EARTH and B-B-B-Benny
and the Jets was on, but no one sang a note.

SOMETHING I DIDN'T WANT TO HEAR

he interrupted my story about my dead lover,
told me to forget about her.
I stopped right there with my tongue
about to lash him into a million little pieces
but instead I remained quiet, with one arm
hanging by my side, my fist shaking
in yet another imaginary fight
when she holds my fist back
as I try to breathe, breathe, breathe
in order to forget the love she left behind
with me in a world where people tell me
I don't even know what love is.

CREEPY OLD GUY

young lovers stop making out
underneath the stars
when they see me staring at them
longing for my own personal romance,
the guy getting up to threaten me
and I tell him that violence
is not the answer but he pummels me
after I admit how hot I thought his
girlfriend was, and I whispered
from the asphalt with blood oozing
down my double chins that
he was such a lucky guy
for winning her heart while mine
pumped faster than premature ejaculate
in fear of this young hunk of burning love
and he kicked me so hard in the scrotum
that I sounded like Mickey Mouse
on helium for weeks after,
unsure if I would ever get lucky again.

GERARD DEPARDIEU

my roommate
smokes a cigarette
and attempts
to impersonate
a French actor
whose name
we kept repeating
out loud in our
obnoxious attempts
to speak with
a French accent
before sunrise,
and that's when
one of our other
roommates poked
his head out the
window after
we woke him
and everybody
in the neighborhood
up. He looked
down on us
on the patio
of our sober living
and he said
pardon my French,
but you two need
to shut the fuck up.

THAT LITTLE SHIT THINKS
SHE KNOWS EVERYTHING

she's twelve years younger than me
and far smaller in size. but she knows
more than I've ever studied.
she's a spitfire manic depressive
alcoholic who blames me
for every little thing,
and she blackmails me
with a series of pictures
taken of me in my underwear
that she threatens to show
our group therapist
and shrink me down
to size even tinier than her.
no one will hear me
when they crush me
underneath their feet
and she wins
the whole damn argument.
that little shit diagnoses
all of the little goddamn things
she thinks are wrong with me.

SOCIAL DISTANCE

I have no children,
am divorced
and I've got
a dead girlfriend.
I do not go to parties
because they all ask me
why I have no job,
and why I have no kids
and please don't make them
feel uncomfortable
before they are drunk
enough to act like
they are listening
when I discuss
my mental illness
and the fact
that I'm a fair weather
friend of Bill W.,
which spoils their fun
so I don't go
to parties anymore
because I am
too afraid I will
want to throw
a one-man party
beyond midnight
while they all sleep,
safe and sound
and unaware

of the sinister side
of me lurking among
shadow demons
in search of a light
that will lead me
back to them
before they all
wake up and notice
that I've been gone.

DOUBLE SCRUB

It started when I was growing up
with a neat freak mother
all those Tuesday's when she blamed
her drill sergeant personality switch on PMS
and forced me to help her scrub out the filth
until I could see my ten year old reflection in it
same thing in rehab twenty years later
and putting up with a hard ass needle hype
as a counselor all of those dreaded Sundays
making it all look immaculate, every inch of it
and on to sober living in the free world
but not so fast double scrub Sundays
when I wanted to leave town for a motel
with my girlfriend
but fuck you, Ridgeway
make it all look brand new and clean
just like you have always needed it to be.

ERASED BY NOSTALGIA

My Uncle Mike told me to stop
looking in the rear view mirror
and hit the gas forward,
the only sensible way
to live free of my demons
and he drops me off
on a Long Beach street corner,
at the end of the day
I said goodbye
to my childhood home
and found myself
in the cold ghetto
of my adulthood,
never to look back again
at what made it all so full
of such mournful promise.

IN HIS OWN LITTLE WORLD

his sonic boom announcer's voice
startles me at every turn of phrase
he employs with endless details
of obscure references,
a computer malfunction
in his mind while he struggles
to make connections between
every single person,
place and thing he references
like a haywire encyclopedia
and all of it makes perfect
schizophrenic sense to him.
I look out my bedroom window,
his voice unmistakable
as he jabbers on to
our speechless landlord
about things nobody
has ever heard of while
I laugh to myself, because
I've heard it all before.

QUARANTINE #9

I am in a screaming match
with the motherfucker next door
both of us mad dogging each other
from windows in locked down houses
across from each other, bored
and paranoid and half naked.
we promise each other
if the world doesn't
come to an end,
we are going to fuck
each other up because
my Amazon Prime order
was delivered to him
by mistake, and to be
extra careful, he will not
give it to me because
of the possibility of
spreading infection,
and I can swear
I hear him watching
the movies I ordered
for myself as a way
to escape from
assholes like him.

THE MOST NOTORIOUS
STREET CORNER IN LONG BEACH, CA

She asked me from her seat between two parked cars
adjacent to a burned out laundromat if I was afraid of black lips,
her African American attitude an authentic kind of sass
which gave birth to rock n roll before white people stole it.
She lit a broken piece of glass and upon exhalation
with a helium voice told me I was sexy before I knew it,
she kissed me and blew all of the crack smoke into my mouth
and I exhaled it all through my nose. I felt nothing but a fast
beating heart and a broken mind. She had to go hustle
for five minutes in order to pick up another rock.
She insisted that we must get nasty wet later on,
when the streets became dark and void of the safety
of common decency, when she hoped to share with me
her deranged ideas, twisted dreams and warped memories.
I murmured an inaudible shit, having forgotten to go
in for group therapy where everyone smelled like
cheap laundry detergent and came equipped
with a stained discount store Cheeto-mustache
and minds which were never or were no longer
warped by street drugs that I sampled in their absence,
having stolen my cheap thrill that day from a woman
who I broke my promise of an alleyway fuck to
when I ran east on Pacific Coast Highway
on my way to the more affluent part of town,
in neighborhoods where I hid out most days
when I wasn't trying to fool pushers, pimps
and ho's into giving me a free hit or two with
a glimpse behind their eyes into a world full
of those of us who all lost our souls when
we thought we had all become free spirits.

IF I EVER SEE MY FATHER AGAIN

The first question
I plan on asking my father
is how he dealt
with my mother's death
while sentenced to life in prison,
his experience now valuable to me
after the death of my girlfriend
made us both widowers of sorts.
I will re-read his last letter
where he claimed to be clean
off drugs for five years
my mother and I didn't get
to spend with him,
and at this darkened hour
I will ask my father
how he managed
to stay clean after
my mother's death
because I have
been struggling since
my girlfriend
drank herself to death
and need to perform
a miraculous
and fractured redemption.
I will whisper my
forgiveness to him
so the rest of the world
cannot hear me ask him
to show me how to live.

PRETTY BOY SLUMLORD

twitches to the side of his neck
when he speaks to me about
smoking pot while living under
the roof of his wet sober living
where people swig methadone
and inject speed on the side
but he gives me a fucking hard
time for trying to forget all the
back rent he's never going to
repay me because he's got an
in with the big boys downtown
as he calls it, twirling his curls
like a fractured washed up old
Adonis in search of new prey,
and he leaves with the pretty
young social worker so I can
finish putting my trousers on.

STRANGE RUMINATION

I am going to break free from this prison
that I built from twisted blueprints,
it's ramshackle facade collapsing over me
like a Buster Keaton near
death experience. I will no longer
befriend isolation, because isolation
feeds me too many bad ideas,
most of which I've kept to myself.
I will no longer stare out the window
at other kids while they all become
close, lifelong friends and I am dragged
further away than any man or woman
has gone before, through the same
black hole my mother entered
when she tried to start a riot
with the blade of her cutting words
but her self-destructive quest for justice
enslaved her and me, a lonesome spirit
who doesn't believe in a god
to perform miracles because
that would make the world a fair
and balanced place where they would
embrace my individuality.
But I'm still here, stigmatized
and staring out of the same old window,
passing notes with poems
written on them in chicken scratch
underneath the front door
no one knocks on any more,
out there in a world of freedom
where I can see everyone but me.

SALLY WITH THE ACCENT

she's from Yonkers
has white skin
white hair
and a bright smile
she used to do social work
and her insight means
she can finish our
therapist's sentences
and initiates
the growing
process
of others
so much
until she stops
responding to her name
but she denies
everything
into the fog
of disassociation
and she woke up lost,
not knowing
where and how
she's found
herself again

.

TIMOTHY

rides the van to
our group therapy,
saying hello, I love you
to every other patient
who climbs aboard
his hand raised
in a tall wave
a plastic smile
spread out
across his doll-like face
before it collapses
into a blank expression
and returns
to the xeroxed
scripture
he studies
everyday
when he's not
crossing
any boundaries
by telling other
men how handsome
they are
and how much
he'd love
to fuck us all.

BUTTHEADS

Cesar and Little Man beg for cigarettes
without any shame during our breaks
before and after our therapy groups
at the outpatient hospital downtown,
smoking discarded butts on the ground
when they are desperate. When they
ask Don Juan for one, he tells them
he wouldn't give them a nickel
to put cheese on a Whopper.
a psychiatrist enters the gate
and steps on a particularly juicy
menthol Newport on the ground
and it sticks to his loafer, which
they chase into the building,
ready to steal it away for a puff
that would make them
feel like a million bucks
upon extraction before they are
both screamed at by the attending
nurse for bothering the poor doctor,
and they then overturn the
butt cans in search of stogies
among spent, toasted filters
that they will never, ever find.

TWO CHICKS AT THE SAME TIME

It was after an N.A. meeting
when we'd all relapsed,
me and two Mexican girls
who removed my pants
but I refused to perform
without a rubber, so we
called the whole thing off
and the fatter of my two
new friends cut a weak
fart she was trying
to hold in. We laid
there until morning,
birds chirping a
guilty verdict while
we wasted our lives
in a feverish desperation
to get our rocks off
that has left us feeling
sexy as garbage cans.

THERAPY REJECT

I lied to my fourth therapist,
telling her all of my bogus
achievements while she jotted
them down on a pad in her lap,
hoping that she couldn't smell
the Schnapps on my breath or
catch me while I admired her
legs during my feeble attempts
to lie to her about my ongoing
drug use so I could remain
her "favorite patient" because
I had finished some college
where I had failed to learn
how to be a good liar.   She
booked an appointment for
the following week that I
would be too hungover to
attend, let alone cancel.
One of the receptionists
walked in on my desperate
attempts at masturbation in
the lobby bathroom in order
to let me know the patient
van had arrived to drive me
and all the other impotent
losers home, or at least to
a quiet place where I could
feel suicidal until I bored
myself into a fourteen hour

coma of too many nightmares
and not enough dreams ready
to come true until I was
ready to come true.

MIDNIGHT HUSTLE

the drug dealer screams at me:
this ain't no game, bitch--
I got a right mind to
whoop your ass
right here in the gutter
but I scream fuck you homie!
and run across the intersection,
threatening to call the police
which gets him to bark harder
and I yell never mind,
I won't call the police,
please don't kill me
while a tripped-out dude
dances five steps forward,
five steps back over and over again
in a broken dance in front of me
while he blasts his walkman
full of old school jams over by
where VIP Records used to be,
all of it rich in music history,
but now its a vacant strip mall
for white boys to run across
in search of other white boys
who ran from the same
hardened men who were
all mistaken when they claimed
we owed them money from
previous drug deals none
of us could remember.

SHE WORE HER HAIR DOWN

we were across the street
from the taco bell we dined
in when we first moved to this city,
both of us in the shadow of death
with the desperation for
a better life in dirty clothes,
both of us giving each other shit
for her drinking and
for my drugging until
my drug kicked in before hers
and she had to carry me over
to the bus stop. she never
wore her hair down since
the night we fell in love,
but she did that day. I do
not remember if we kissed
each other goodbye or
if I hugged her when she
whispered to me final words
that I lost in a deep narcotic
sleep in my bed at home.
she kept trying to call me
through the night because
something was wrong
and I listened to her voice
in the messages she recorded
her quiet, inaudible voice dying
when I failed to carry her back
to the safety of our broken love.

DEADBEAT CLAIRVOYANT

My father broke the silence
between us by declaring
in a handwritten letter
from state prison
that I have
genetic heart disease
just like him
and my hillbilly grandfather
before him. My father
has not seen me in ten years.
How does he know
my future diagnosis?
He urged me to get
my heart checked because
I am going to die of this
sudden family tradition
he's sprung upon me.
He must know the future,
because he created me
from out of his lazy scrotum
and often writes of this fact
in his letters to his
one and only son.
I wonder if my father
can appreciate these
sloppy metaphors of mine
as I try to reach across
the bars of his cell in order
to shake him good and hard
with each and every
last one of them.

SOFT HANDS

my long soft hands
have never worked a day
in their lives
other than to sign
welfare checks
and jack off
in the bathrooms
at my relatives
and friends'
houses
ever since
I got kicked out
of my mother's
house when she
died and we had
to sell it, all that
hard work of hers
gone totally to
waste, off the clock
and bloody in the
knuckles and in
her blue eyes
that closed
whenever I read
her one of my poems.

THE UNIVERSE IS EXPANDING

The world is moving faster and faster toward
optimum mindfulness and a kind of cyber focus that
I fall out of line with, the games and the selfies and
the applications that have transformed me into a
21st Century Luddite, cruising from the waves of the
archives my elders left behind for me to lose myself
as an Indiana Jones seeker of admiring girls, teaching
college to the hip sexy kids while I chase down the
ark of the covenant, in my case a poem that's better
than any woman I've ever fucked, superior to any
chill down my spine at the end of a film I've never
forgotten after all these years. I'm not afraid of girls
anymore. They're afraid of me.

WILD OATS

She stopped fucking me,
told me I needed to fuck
more people than I'd fucked
in my lifetime. She did it,
and everyone else did it.
So why the holdup on my end?
She decided to go and die on me,
leaving me with no choice
but to find somebody else to fuck
who will give me shit
for not fucking more people
until the human race
goes extinct from
my lack of fucking,
not a single baby
will be fucked
into existence--they'd
be lost causes just like me.
But she's dead and so
is the majority of my family,
which means they can see me
down here, in a world
where even the dead
are getting laid, but not me.

KODAK MOMENT

Whenever he got high,
Dad would trip out
on the fact that
he created me
from out of his scrotum
while we passed
the tin foil of heroin
between each other.
He shook his head
and intoned in a deep,
scary voice that he was
my demented master.

HE TOLD HIMSELF
A JOKE HE HADN'T
HEARD BEFORE

He has enough time on
his unemployable hands
to spoon feed himself
Luck Charms at noon,
silence all around him
with no one to entertain.
so he became his
own number one fan,
a demented king
of hallucinatory
comedy, laughing
at things no one
else will ever be
able to understand.

CARTOON VIOLENCE

I am sitting here on Black Friday in my underwear,
watching a little girl slaughter a gang of thieves and
    murderers
with goofy sound effects painted in Technicolor gore.
Everyone is dead and I have to return to the old drawing
    board
nestled in my skull on how to reach out from the bars of
    my cell
for another source of love as I forget to laugh at something
I don't find so funny anymore
after the birth of a long and lonesome new era of silent TNT
ready to self destruct in a split second of a false move at chess
with the Reaper himself with the hope for a Wile E. Coyote
Acme-bought arsenal of fearsome immortality.

FATALISTIC LONG BEACH POEM

I'm waiting for the bus alone
on Pacific Coast Highway
to ride to group therapy
where I'll tell them I'm fine
and some blowhard family intern
asks me to elaborate
in a way that insults my intelligence
and I tell him I feel alone in the world
that everyone abandoned me
for a better life
with new love
that this old love keeps me from finding
ghetto scum boulevards
remind me of the stink of wasted minds
like this one
as it formulates a bullshit response
that he jots down
for insurance purposes.

MY UBER DRIVER GETS IT

I climbed into the passenger's seat
and told the elderly woman
behind the wheel
who asked me
how I am doing
that I was "hanging in there"
she waited a beat
as she merged into traffic
before she claimed
that I stole her line
and to keep hanging in there.
she said life can be very difficult
and her weary eyes met mine
in the rear view mirror
to offer me a slice of wisdom
trembling out of the gushing
blood of her humanity.

ICE CREAM & METHADONE

he took me to that parking lot
filled with lost souls and half-empty cups
disappearing beneath the flash of a fluorescent light
as he opened the security door
having coming back more awake than I had ever seen him
he brought a friend, who took the wheel
and to Skid Row we went
over to meet his man, who drove a black Cadillac
we did the junk in the back seat of his Honda
and then his fellow patient drove us home
we slurped on Jack in the Box single scoop ice creams,
his chocolate, mine vanilla
we pushed our cones together to create
a double drip flavor effect for one another
and then we both nodded off,
headed east back to the suburbs
our closed eyelids facing the fading skyline
of Los Angeles and its stacks of
orange smog cloud fuming scrapers
our bodies and brains fighting
for oxygen and the meaning of our lives
two extinguished cigarettes still
smoldering in half-eaten cones
two half-dead bodies baking underneath
the back shield waiting for redemption.

SEMI-ANNUAL DETOX

the semi-annual detox is in full swing,
water, vitamins, minerals and codeine
clutter the fold-out TV tray with bent legs
leaning against the rumpled man's bed
The one-eyed cat has more muscle than you
he sinks his claws into your bulging stomach
and winks with his good eye,
the empty socket a vibrating red void
You get up and struggle to the food nook
the cat is still attached to your mid section
you fix him a morsel of juicy wet chunks
nestled in-between your flapping sugared udders
You bite open a powdered beverage with electrolytes,
adolescent crack that you stir with your
pinkie finger in a jiffy of lower middle class self-help
still-dry flavor crystals bedazzling your upper lip hair
Time for a horrible endless reel
of Lifetime Movies for Grandma
the entertainment bulbs in the box glow
while you piss yourself in the dark.

THE MOST BEAUTIFUL WOMAN
IN THE WORLD

stammering in my drunkenness,
my tuxedo shirt drenched in cabernet
I tried to carry on awkward conversations
with all of the other wedding guests
but they shunned me, called me "sloppy boy"
I smeared my face with cake and wanted to cry
and then she appeared from the raining city outside
fashionably late, having other commitments
underdressed in her street clothes in the midst
of evening gowns, pressed suits and perfume
she had gone to school with my brother
and recognized my elfin face, busted
blood vessels and all, sobbing in the corner
she asked me how the wedding went
and I told her she was the
most beautiful woman in the world,
and a pregnant pause was wedged between us
I dropped my pants and began to dance
the Charleston in front of her and everyone
in eye view, repeating my praise of her
and then urinated on the sidewalk outside
pictures were taken; I was ushered off to rehab
while she went on to star in films and television
she would appear on the cover of a magazine
the reporter writing the article called her
"the most beautiful woman in the world"
at least I was right about something that night.

A YOUNG SOCIAL WORKER TEACHES
ME ABOUT MEDICARE

I lost my temper
with the young girl
behind the glass
at the social security office
when she transformed me
into a big idiot for not
understanding Medicare
and she scolded me
for staring at her legs
before her age came out
in her attempts to stifle
her high-pitched laughter
at a loser who wasted
her precious time
in search of a help
I have always been
too afraid to ask for.

ON TOP AGAIN

I had been evicted
from my home for
perpetual drunkenness;
my father-in-law
had choked me in a
whiskey-soaked
fight and I sounded
like Tom Waits
for weeks after,
chain-smoking
Newport's and
wasting my
unemployment
checks on
cocaine &
beer,
squatting
indefinitely in
a section 8
apartment
complex
I found a plastic
dollar store hat
in the dumpster
behind the
Salvation Army
that said
"On Top Again"
across the front

to boost my
spirits, I marched
around with that
hat on my head, but
I wasn't fooling a
soul, including
my own.

.

.

YOU'RE WORTH IT, SO WORK IT

I got high all winter,
and am sitting here in
a meeting overlooking
a yacht club with
three dozen geezers
and one hot, short-
skirted chick passing
around a collection
basket. They all tell
me to keep coming
back after I stand up
to introduce myself
and my disease
to them, and the
whole room laughs
after the leader
admonishes me
for speaking out
of turn. Tey all
tell the same
coffee burnt
stories of
inglorious
demoralization
while I sit there
and begin to
slowly ignore
them in a
day old glaze.

I've got a new song
in my head, and
I don't care if anyone
else is listening.

APPENDIX SCAR

it smiles faintly,
partially obscured
underneath the
waist band
of the tease
of my partially
exposed boxer shorts
when she asks
if she can look at it
and she is impressed
with a blush, a giggle
and an oh my lord
before she gives
it kisses across
it's sealed mouth,
a pain that had
finally begun to
have been worth it.

MINDFULNESS TRAINING

will not help me
when i am swishing
a gin and tonic
around in my mouth
to notice the flavor
and sensation
before i swallow
it and pray for
the effect
that numbs
me to this
mind and
the endless
bullshit
that it's
full of.

COMFORT FOR THE LIVING

if she could only see and hear us now!
but the universe tends to unravel
as it should, all of its cosmic meaning
is beyond human comprehension.
she will never be nothing.
even though I saw her empty shell
over my brother's shoulder
as he asked me where we should
have body that carried us both sent.
It was a beautiful vessel which,
carried me into this life.
she is the beginning
of all I've ever known.
her strength is what keeps me
from worrying about her
out there in the cosmos--
she was afraid of nothing
and she was afraid of no one,
including you and you and you!
I wish she would have
sat upright in that busy
intensive care unit so
she could have her
rightful last words
but I hear what
they are everyday
when I see her in the
reflection of my face.
I realize she never died

because her legacy
still sings to me,
a broken record
I never want fixed.

WE CLEAN UP GOOD

The old Mexican lady showed us
the laundry bill for the formal outfits
we wore on that day when my brother
told her we were running late
for our mother's funeral.
the old Mexican lady froze into place
and performed the sign of the cross.
She tore up the bill, and insisted
that her services for us in our dark hour
were free of charge. My brother
tried to stop her but she interrupted
in Spanish before holding her hand
in front of her tears as she told us
to look our best and to make our
mother prouder of us than she was
when she was still alive, still folding
our laundry and still shaking her head.

MY OLD DRUG DEALER

He smiles ear to ear
across Cherry Avenue
at the 7 Eleven,
ready for me
to buy
some crystal
which he paws
into the palm
of my hand.
I flick it with
a finger steady
enough to claim
nine months
off dope.
I tell him
I'm clean now,
but he thinks
I'm full of shit.
He stands there
in the fizzled glow
of an empty,
burned out laundromat,
waiting for me to fall
so he can swoop
in and catch me.

CLEANING HELGA'S GRAVE

My grandmother's Swedish mother
was run over by a car in 1932,
flattened out of existence
after the family moved to California.
We found an old photograph of them
standing over her grave with the words
written in cursive on the backside.
My grandmother had started
to develop dementia, so we had
to move fast. She told us what
she could remember about
her mother's death in tears
of confusion and fear at how long
her mother had been dead.
My mother and I blazed down
the 5 Freeway to Forest Lawn
with my grandma in the back seat.
We found a large green hill known
as the Sunrise Slope near
a mausoleum where Hollywood
legends rest in eternal silence.
We saw the headstone
and helped my grandmother
walk halfway down the steep hill
until she sat down on the grass
next to the grave, exasperated
until she saw her mother's name
and the vintage, old world light
in her eyes became flooded

by her tears before I made
a funny face to cheer her up
enough to find herself
behaving like a grandmother again,
telling me in her gentle whisper
to smile for once, before she added
that she could never take me anywhere.

WAKING UP IN THE DARK

I walk into a morning bathed
in the flicker of street lights
prior to the false hope
of a new dawn. I'm among
drug addicts, drug dealers
and prostitutes, never to give
them my money again,
money I intend to spend at 7-11
on coffee and an overpriced pack
of Chesterfields, two things
I enjoy while sitting
on a curb and writing
poems in the gutter,
where everything
has gotten to be too real
for me as I watch the world
slowly tumble apart
all around me. I had
begun to discover myself
for the first time, like
a talent agent who was going
to make himself the biggest star
in the world. A homeless
woman sits down next to me
on a bus stop bench and asks me
if I have any shit she can smoke.
I tell her never again would
I be lost in the fog
of a paranoid howl

in the alleyways she still
ran up and down
as we become illuminated
by the sun in order to see
the dirty truth all around us
so I can rub it into a weary
and forgotten prayer.

THE LAST PICTURE SHOW

In the courthouse holding cell,
an OG told me his brother
told him that this life is no movie,
and it doesn't have to end like one.

Then he told me to stay out of trouble
and out of the movies.

THE IMPOSSIBILITY OF ANGELS

He stood on the northwest
corner of Tenth and Atlantic,
facing the front porch of the house
she took her last breath in,
closer than ever to
where her doom came
in a gruesome night
he kept playing in his head
over and over again.
He saw the house
from across the street
every day out the window
of his drug dealer's apartment
until the day he decided
to stop throwing himself away.
He stood there with
a clearing head just as
a beat up old Camaro
turned the corner,
playing her favorite song
while he began to reach
with tremulous hands
to repair a broken sky.

TIME IS RUNNING OUT AND THERE'S NO HAPPINESS

His regrets left tears
on the first page
of his letter on prison stationary,
guilty for not being there for me
and for being an asshole
who only cared about drugs.
He lost my mother forever
and he and I nearly lost each other
during a time of silence
when he saved my life
from becoming cold and bitter.
That's when he told me
that I was the greatest thing
to ever come out of his
and my mother's love,
misspelled words that saved my life
out here with the burden of freedom,
in pursuit of an elusive happiness
beyond the prison walls
that hide him from me and me from him
as I decide to give us both another chance.

MY GIRLFRIEND KISSED MR. ROGERS

He was the first man I trusted and loved
in the wake of my father's disappearance
from my life. He wore a cardigan I envied.
He was a smooth operator who never
let me down and her loving spirit
complimented his as they killed everyone
with the same relentless kindness
that killed them both. She embraced
the gentle public television star
onstage after he spoke
at her college graduation,
and she whispered lusty poetry
into his ear before she surprised him
with a kiss. They were joined together
in a force field of an electric goodness
so potent they could have used it to
save the world. She left me
for Mr. Rogers, who she followed
into a cosmic neighborhood
somewhere in a great beyond
where they earned
an impossible sainthood.
The compassionate lip-lock
she initiated years ago
still haunts my wildest daydreams,
where I can hear her whisper
"won't you be mine?"

THE LORD'S DAY

That's what she called Sundays
when we drank wine and watched
old movies on television,
Robert Mitchum our patron diablo
with a desperate soundtrack
yelled out of Warren Zevon's lungs
her laughter at the ridiculous things
I said and did when I could
be my full tragicomic self
in the company of another sinner
with saucy poetry in her blood
as it pumped into her saintly heart
underneath all the pleasures of the flesh,
a flesh her spirit would one day shed
leaving me alone here on the lord's day
in search of the kind of trouble
that made me fall in love.

Kevin Ridgeway is the author of the previous collection *Too Young to Know* (Stubborn Mule Press, 2019) and several chapbooks of poetry. His work has appeared in *Slipstream, Chiron Review, Nerve Cowboy, Main Street Rag, San Pedro River Review, Trailer Park Quarterly, The Cape Rock, Plainsongs, Into the Void, Book of Matches, Cultural Daily* and *The American Journal of Poetry,* among others. A Pushcart Prize and Best of the Net nominee, he lives and writes in Long Beach, CA.